MW01227187

INTENTIONAL CHRISTIANITY

AUTHOR: The Holy Spirit

INSTRUMENT: Alex Bess

Dedication...

For many years I struggled with
comprehending the Christian faith
mainly because there were few role
models that I personally knew who
practiced what they preached. I am
sorry to say that even though I
grew up in the church, I cannot
remember one preacher who made
the kind of impression on me that
would cause me to even consider
ordination of any kind. Fortunately,
once I finally made the
commitment to allow God to use
me exclusively for His plan and
purpose I found it necessary to
embark upon a journey of
discovery which has not yet come
to an end. I have to give proper
respect and admiration to the men
I was introduced to by the Holy
Spirit who helped me to get to

where I am today. Most of these men have one thing in common. They are deceased. But, they still live on in the books they authored that I have read more than once. I praise God for the committed sons of God who helped me to grow in God's grace... Watchman Nee, Dietrich Bonhoeffer, Andrew Murray, Dan Stone, A W Tozer, J.F. Strombeck and William Law to mention a few.

Most recently I have been discipled by pastors Sam Soleyn, and John Glenn. The late pastor William J. Green challenged me to strengthen my relationship with The Father and not to give up that relationship for an incomplete religion. Alex and Vivian Bess raised me and by brother and sister (Charles and Linda) to live by biblical values as they understood them. Dad and mom are now watching from heaven.

I also am grateful for the men in my discipleship class at South Bay and Okeechobee Correctional Institute who have taught me as much as God has given them through me over the past 10 years. Dr. Scott Hearing and the men who attend the Friday morning prayer breakfast and those faithful souls who participate in our weekly study groups have kept me grounded and engaged in God's plan and purpose for my life. And, I praise God for my pastor, John Glenn, who is a friend, brother and encourager. My friend and brother, Jay Bonner, has been on this journey with me for the past ten years and together we have learned to speak the truth in love, to be Christ to others, and to practice what we teach. All of these saints have been, and still are, instrumental in my growth and continued commitment to living the life God has ordained for me.

This book is dedicated to them and to the love of my life, Margaret, who is God's gift to me and His instrument for teaching me how to love.

Introduction....

Teaching is the natural occupation of every living soul. The term "teach" is defined as: to cause to know; to instruct by precept, knowledge and experience; to make known and accepted. This is an action word that applies even to those of us who may be inactive. A medical examiner will tell you that you can learn something from a dead man. We are all teachers whether we are conscious of that fact or not. Adam's Teacher was the Sovereign God of the universe and the creation that He provided. Eve learned from Adam. We learn from each other with every transaction. The only real question is, what are we teaching each other? What are we teaching our children?

Many people equate teaching to a monologue of facts and analogies disseminated by individuals certified to teach a specific subject. That may be true, but it is only a small part of what teaching really is as can be confirmed by most certified teachers. Even though every soul is a teacher not every soul is qualified to teach. I make that statement based on the fact that there are some things that are taught that should not be and they are usually taught by teachers whose genetic state of confusion prevents them from doing otherwise.

The chosen title for this book may sound like a profound revelation that once realized may change the status and condition of the average soul for the better. Intentional Christianity is a radical endeavor that requires one to practice what they teach. The sad truth is that we all operate by faith but most Christians are not intentional in that endeavor. We all are intentional about what we believe even when we unintentionally express those beliefs. Our proclamations of the truth of God's Word are usually not followed up with the application of that truth in our everyday lives. Our daily conversations are motivated by selfish ambition and grounded in confusion that is so common that any communication on a higher level seems ridiculous and peculiar. If we accept the biblical account of creation, we have to believe that the only true standard for sanity and a productive existence is to live according to God's plan and purpose for mankind. Anything else can only result in confusion. Whether we teach truth or error we all practice what we teach and we are all intentional in our dysfunction.

Knowing the Truth is incomplete and unconfirmed without an intentional commitment to becoming the product of that Truth. The transformation process initiated and perpetuated by the Holy Spirit requires an intentional surrender and a radical obedience to God's plan and purpose. The resulting intimate relationship with a loving Heavenly Father is

manifested as we learn how to be
Christ to others.

In the beginning...

A perfect God created a perfect
universe and then a perfect son.
Since God is love, He devised a
plan whereby He would manifest
His love through His creation.
Adam was privileged to be created
in the image of God and through
his relationship with his Father he
would be able to manifest the
character of God in the
environment in which he was
placed. Adam was given dominion
over everything on the earth via
this Father/son relationship. From

God's creation Adam still had a lot to learn but his Teacher would be his Father. The Father would teach His son to manifest His character and maintain order on the earth and that would result in the earth being a reflection of the Kingdom of Heaven. The earth, ruled by the son, would be an extension of the Kingdom and a result of the father/son relationship. God's plan and purpose for His children would become a reality. Pastor Myles Monroe put it this way: "God's plan was to rule the visible from the invisible through the invisible in the visible on the visible."

Just as love must be manifested as proof of its existence, obedience must also be tested as proof of faithfulness. God's created man was given free will and had the

choice to maintain a loving
relationship with his Father or to
disobey His instructions and chose
the forbidden tree. That decision
was prompted by a lie from Satan
and a selfish desire to impress
God. The fatal decision to partake
of the tree of the knowledge of
good and evil severed the divine
relationship necessary for the
peaceful existence of mankind and
the manifestation of God's initial
plan and purpose for man
(sonship). All souls born into this
world after the introduction of sin
were born into the Adams family
and not into the family of God.
Before the fall there was no
confusion or dysfunction. The
simple fact is that even though
man had dominion over the earth,
that authority was given by God

and the exercise of that authority
was possible only because of
Adam's faithful relationship with his
Heavenly Father. God was in
charge and His son, Adam, was
submissive to Him. Adam never
suffered, never experienced want,
and never had any negative
emotions, thoughts, or feelings. His
life was perfect. Adam did not need
to partake of the forbidden tree
because he already had the
knowledge of good. He had a
personal relationship with the
source of everything that is good.
The first couple's only mistake was
wanting to do for themselves what
God had already done for them.
They wanted to impress The Father
by trying to please Him instead of
just trusting Him and depending on
Him only. The only thing that

Adam and Eve could experience for the first time from that forbidden tree was the knowledge of evil and that knowledge is the root of every negative issue, trial, and tribulation mankind experiences today. Once evil (sin) becomes a part of mankind's DNA the only permanent solution to his confusion is death. Death is also the only remedy for his salvation.

The spiritual man that God created has become a soul man because of sin. The natural man is naturally confused about all things because rather than submit to God's plan and purpose for his life he would rather be god or impress The Father with his own efforts to solve the issues of the flesh with the intellectual processes of an ungodly, dysfunctional mind. All the issues of life are spiritual issues and therefore require a spiritual solution. Without the power of the Holy Spirit we are incapable of accessing the right answers because the only right answer is God's answer and dead men walking don't have a relationship with the source of all truth. Confusion ends or begins with making a decision as to who is in control. Sanity is only possible when God is the head of our lives via the Holy Spirit.

Two kinds of confusion...

The introduction of sin meant not only the death of man's spiritual relationship with God but also a consistent deterioration of all of his physical and mental functions. As long as man was functioning according to God's divine order…. spirit, soul, body…. God was in control. Man willingly submitted to that arrangement, and there was no confusion. At the moment that man sinned his eyes were opened, his spirit died, and he became a soul man. Adam and Eve, for the first time, felt shame at their nakedness and tried to cover themselves. This confusion resulted in outright rebellion in the form of the "blame game." We still play that game today in an attempt to defend our condemned flesh. Spiritual death left man dependent upon himself for his provision and protection. Satan's plan was so subtle that men still remain slaves to a world system that leads them to believe that they are in charge. Men struggle and die for sex, money and power while refusing to believe that the prince of the power of the air is a real spiritual being. With every soul born lost and corrupted by sin, the resulting confusion is inevitable. However, men still attempt to rule and reign in the midst of an insanity that is justified by human logic devoid of the Word of God.

In his book, "The Latent Power of the Soul", Watchman Nee gives evidence of the capabilities of mankind without the direction of the Spirit of God. The mind, will, and emotions are the dominant components of the soul of man and mankind has made remarkable achievements in spite of his rebellion against God. Just look around at the world we live in and observe how far we have come. The problem is that none of those things can restore life to humankind. Death is a consequence of sin and it cannot be avoided. You may not have considered this but God was the author of confusion for a humanity that was unified in a state of confusion it was not even aware of. After the fall, men actually believed they could be like God. Satan's lie had taken root and mankind, separated from the Spirit of Truth and controlled by the soul, believed they could figure out the answers to life's issues by themselves. This is still true today. Early man had one advantage. "At one time all the people of the world spoke the same language and used the same words." (Gen. 11:1). The Father/son relationship was no longer a priority and selfishness became the order of the day both individually and corporately. "They began saying to each other, 'Let's make bricks and harden them with fire.' Then they said, 'Come, let's build a great city **for ourselves** with a tower that reaches into the sky. This will **make us famous** and keep **us** from being scattered all over the world.' (Gen.11:3-4)

Even in man's sinful state God's love was evident. His covenant with Himself (Rev.13:8) before the creation of man provided the means for salvation for every soul whether accepted or not. How long does it take for any man to realize that the salvation provided by God through the death and resurrection of Jesus is all we will ever need for eternal, abundant life? God clothed the first couple after they sinned and still provided for them in their independence. He provides for mankind in his rebellion even when his thoughts are totally devoid of God's love for him. "But the Lord came down to look at the city and the tower the people were building. Look! He said. The people are **united**, and they all speak the **same language**. After this, nothing they set out to do will be impossible for them! Come, let's go down and **confuse the people with different languages**. Then they won't be able to understand each other." (Gen.11:5-7) Even in his confusion, caused by sin, man was, and still is, able to use his intellect to accomplish feats and establish a level of existence that will not only allow him to remain comfortable in his sin but brag about what he has done, is doing, and will do in the future. Confusion caused by language is just a temporary setback. All men are dysfunctional idiots, born as slaves to sin and incapable of attaining righteousness without God. The minute we are born we begin to die and the world informs us that we should spend what time we have enjoying ourselves because we cannot save ourselves.

Confusion has become the normal state of mind. Confusion is so subtle and unrecognizable that it is considered the common state of man unless it results in chaos.

"I am the LORD your God, who brought you out of the land of Egypt, out of the house of bondage. You shall have no other gods before Me. You shall not make for yourself a carved image—any likeness of anything that is in heaven above, or that is in the earth beneath, or that is in the water under the earth; you shall not bow down to them nor serve them. For I, the LORD your God, am a jealous God, visiting the iniquity of the fathers upon the children to the third and fourth generations of those who hate Me, but showing mercy to thousands, to those who love Me and keep My commandments." (Ex. 20:1-5)

Since God set the standard for life and peace, only God can provide for the redemption of mankind.

God, in the flesh, died on the cross
for the sins of mankind so that
men would be free to reconcile
with their Heavenly Father and live
eternally as sons of Almighty God.
Confusion is defined medically as a
disturbance of consciousness
characterized by inability to engage
in orderly thought or by lack of
power to distinguish, choose, or act
decisively. It is not until we accept
the Truth and receive a new heart
and a new spirit that we are freed
from the confusion and bondage of
being slaves to sin. The soul must
be saved and it is only when we
are led by the Spirit that we have
clarity about who we are in Christ
and what our Father has planned
for us.

Ignorance of truth is perpetuated by those who are either ignorant of the truth or refuse to accept it.

RIGHT OR WRONG?

This question never was asked before Adam and Eve partook of the tree of the knowledge of good and evil. The concept of wrong was never a consideration because of God's personal relationship with the man He created. Since God is always good (and right) everything He does is always good (and right). The created son, Adam, lived to please his Father and never allowed his curiosity to stray farther than that desire. Adam's question to God was never "why" but "Father, what do you want me to do?"

The question of why do you want me to do this is rooted in ignorance and fear as a result of a severed relationship with the source of all truth. This is because when God is our source the "why" question is answered by the "what" question. Adam was created perfect but not complete. There was a maturing process that was necessary and his relationship with his Father would provide everything he needed for the completion of that ongoing process. That spiritual relationship would not only teach him to become a mature son of God but would be passed on to his children as he obeyed the command to be fruitful and multiply. His obedience to and love for his heavenly Father should have even prevented the inevitable fall.

Once sin was allowed into the created world the alternative to spiritual growth and maturity became more and more attractive because it fed the selfish desire of mankind to "be like God." This is still complicated by a misconception of who God is.

Before the fall man's soul (mind, will, and emotions) was submissive to his spirit. Adam was a spiritual man because of the Father/son relationship between him and Almighty God. Man was designed to be dependent upon his heavenly Father as his source for provision, protection, and glory. Like any good Father, God delights in raising and providing for His children and gets all the glory from watching them mature into responsible sons and daughters.

When man sinned that relationship was severed and Adam became a soul man. Every child of Adam now thinks independently of God and even when accepting the truth elects to please and impress God by his own efforts rather than obediently follow His instructions. His soul is so corrupt that it needs to be saved from the hell and death it deserves. The insanity that exist in the physical world is so common that the truth, even when acknowledged, is not only difficult to accept but is often rejected by those who refuse to give up their gods for the one true God. We are convinced that we can save ourselves without God's help. So we become religious enemies of each other rather than brothers "in Christ."

My brothers, if you are married you are already aware that there are three answers to every dilemma...the right answer, the wrong answer and your wife's answer. If you have been married for more than a day you also have discovered that your wife's answer is always the right answer. When it comes to the rest of the world my right is always right and your wrong is always wrong. Because we are naturally self-centered and selfish we always want to be right. The problem is that because we are all independent thinkers we all have our own concept of what right is. So, we are not really seeking the right answer but confirmation from those who agree with our decision as to what that answer is. Until we come to the knowledge that there is only one right and that everything else is wrong we will never agree with each other. Until we agree with God we will never agree with each other because until our answer is His answer we can only agree on the wrong answer no matter how right it sounds.

The character of Christ can only be manifested through a man who has died and been reborn. The spiritual man is a new creation who is not subject to religion but led by the Spirit of God. The life of Christ is manifested through him in such a way that when men see him they see Jesus. They see a son of God being used by God to do His good will and complete His plan and purpose. They see someone who is willing and available to serve as

both a king and a priest in every situation and empowered by the Holy Spirit to do so. For the child of God there is no right or wrong, there is only the question..."
Father, what do you want me to do in this situation?"

All of our human drama is either initiated or perpetrated by our desire to be right in our own eyes.

RADICAL CHRISTIANITY...

Because of God's grace we have the FREEDOM to love others as Christ loved us. Freedom is often misunderstood. It is not a matter of physical location but PERCEPTION. True freedom is reserved only for those who are "in Christ."

"So now there is no
condemnation for those who
belong to Christ Jesus. And
because you belong to Him, the
power of the life-giving Sprit
has freed you from the power
of sin that leads to death. The
law of Moses was unable to
save us because of the
weakness of our flesh. So God
did what the law could not do.
He sent His Own Son in a body
like the bodies we sinners
have. And in that body God
declared an end to sin's control
over us by giving His Son as a
sacrifice for our sins. He did
this so that the just
requirement of the law would
be fully satisfied for us, who no
longer follow our flesh but

**instead follow the Spirit."
(Rom. 8:1-4)**

For the most part, we have accepted a watered down gospel or only half the gospel and have spent most of our lives as Christians stuck in Romans 7. Even though saved, we still live our lives in the flesh while striving to improve ourselves and be good Christians. The reality of the true gospel is that God has already done for us what we could not do for ourselves through the death and resurrection of Jesus. By the power of His Holy Spirit we CAN live the life He has ordained for each and every one of us. It is only when we accept the Truth that we can see the reality of God's plan and purpose.

Culture informs perspective. It is only through "new birth" that we can see the Kingdom of God. The culture of the Kingdom is difficult to understand because we were all raised in the cultures of the world. A flawed model influenced by a physical understanding prevents a true interpretation and vision of the existing invisible Kingdom of God. This multicultural world that we live in is not only confusing but our human efforts to correct our confusion breeds even more dysfunction. Even when we come to the realization that the culture of the Kingdom of God is the only solution for peace and harmony our innate selfishness prevents us from accepting that truth.

True freedom is only available via the Gospel of Jesus the Christ.

"Jesus told him. 'I am the way, the truth, and the life. No one can come to the Father except through me." (Jn.14:6) It is only through our acceptance of the truth of God's Word that we can all experience the peace that surpasses all understanding. The core issue of our personal problems is traced back to the false assumptions we hold concerning what it takes to make us secure and significant (worthy). Every living soul has the desire to be loved and is primarily focused on that objective. We all make judgments and determine the state of our relationships by our evaluation of whether or not we "feel" loved. What we fail to realize is that our understanding of the concept of love is dysfunctional because it is impossible for the soul that does not KNOW God to love. God is love and divine love is only accessible through Him. Since it is impossible to love without a personal relationship with Almighty God, it is also impossible to love others without Him. In reality, God loves through us because we cannot. One must receive God's love before one can love others. Since it is our nature to "feel" important and significant and adequate it is also necessary for us to be able to give that which we desire to receive. Through the death and resurrection of Jesus we accept, by faith, the love and acceptance and forgiveness of the sovereign God of the universe.

The world system offers us everything except eternal life. Even though we accept the inevitability of death we do everything we can to avoid that certainty. We spend billions to look like we are not dying physically. Then we spend thousands on a dead relative to insure that they don't look dead at the funeral. We constantly are engaged in a personal pursuit to make ourselves feel good, look good, and be good. We become frustrated when we cannot afford the things we want even though we have everything we need. Our false assumptions about what it takes to make us safe and secure and significant are so natural that it is difficult to even recognize, much less trust, the biblical assumptions concerning our worth as spiritual beings created by God. Our failure to recognize Almighty

God as the source of our provision, protection and our very lives is the primary reason for all our dysfunction. The indoctrination of the world system and the natural tendency of the flesh results in the rejection of God's plan and purpose by those who would rather be God than serve Him. Even those who accept the truth struggle with total surrender and commitment to the Spirit of Life by trying to please Him in their own power (Rom. 7).

THE NATURAL CONDITION OF MAN….

According to the first three chapters of Romans the natural condition of man is that of a dysfunctional, useless, hopeless sinner. The truth is that all men are born into a dysfunctional humanity that can be identified as the family of Adam. The verdict is that our only hope for redemption is death and resurrection. Salvation is necessary and available to one who is willing to die and be reborn into the family of God. "As the scriptures say, **'No one is righteous—not even one. No one is truly wise; no one is seeking God. All have turned away; all have become useless. No one does good, not a single one. Their talk is foul, like the stench from an open grave. Their tongues are filled with lies. Snake venom drips from their lips. Their mouths are full of cursing and bitterness. They rush to commit murder. Destruction and misery always**

follow them. They don't know where to find peace. They have no fear of God at all.' Obviously, the law applies to those to whom it was given, for its purpose is to keep people from having excuses, and to show that the entire world is guilty before God. For no one can ever be made right with God by doing what the law commands. The law simply shows us how sinful we are." (Rom.3:10-20) There is no hope for the soul that will not admit that we CANNOT change ourselves but we need a Savior.

There is Good News. "For I am not ashamed of this Good News about Christ. It is the power of God at work, saving everyone who believes—the Jew first and also the

Gentile. This Good News tells us how God makes us right in His sight. This is accomplished from start to finish by faith. As the Scriptures say, 'It is through faith that a righteous person has life." (Rom. 1:16-17) "But now God has shown us a way to be made right with Him without keeping the requirements of the law, as was promised in the writings of Moses and the prophets long ago. We are made right with God by placing our faith in Jesus Christ. And this is true for everyone who believes, no matter who we are.

For everyone has sinned; we all fall short of God's glorious standard. Yet God freely and graciously declares that we are righteous. He did this through Christ Jesus when He freed us from the penalty for our sins. For God presented Jesus as the sacrifice for sin. People are made right with God when they believe that Jesus sacrificed His life, shedding His blood. This sacrifice shows that God was being fair when he held back and did not punish those who sinned in times past, for He was looking ahead and including them in what He would do in this present time. God did this to demonstrate His righteousness, for He Himself is fair and just, and He declares sinners to be right in His sight when they believe in Jesus.

Can we boast, then, that we have done anything to be accepted by God? No, because our acquittal is not based on obeying the law. It is based on faith. So we are made right with God through faith and

not by obeying the law. "
(Rom.3:21-28)

NEW BIRTH...

No matter who you are, what you
have, where you were born...no
matter what your situation, you
can start over. Our provision, our
protection, our security and
significance, our worth comes as a
free gift when we receive the
righteousness of Christ. This is
God's righteousness...a
righteousness that has never
sinned, is not now sinning and will
never sin. This righteousness
cannot be earned by the sinful,
dysfunctional flesh but can be
received BY FAITH apart from
works (justification). "For the

wages of sin is death, but the free gift of God is eternal life through Christ Jesus our Lord." (Rom.6:23) God's righteousness is available to every living soul who will accept it. "So we have stopped evaluating others from a human point of view. At one time we thought of Christ merely from a human point of view. How differently we know Him now. This means that anyone who belongs to Christ has become a new person. The old life is gone; a new life has begun." (2 Cor.5:16-17)

The divine, eternal life of Christ is only available to those who, by the power of the Holy Spirit, experience "new birth." When we personally trust in the fact that Jesus died for us, we automatically, and without reservation or revocation, receive the righteousness of God. "Once you were dead because of your disobedience and your many sins. You used to live in sin, just like the rest of the world, obeying the devil—the commander of the powers in the unseen world. He is the spirit at work in the hearts of those who refuse to obey God. All of us used to live that way, following the passionate desires and inclinations of our sinful nature. By our very nature we were subject to God's anger, just like everyone else. '

'But God is so rich in mercy, and He loved us so much, that even though we were dead because of our sins, He gave us life when He raised Christ from the dead. (It is only by God's grace that you have been saved!) For He raised us from the dead along with Christ and seated us with Him in the heavenly realms because we are united with Christ Jesus. So God can point to us in all future ages as examples of the incredible wealth of His grace and kindness toward us, as shown in all He has done for us who are united with Christ Jesus.'

'God saved you by His grace when you believed. And you can't take credit for this; it is a gift from God. Salvation is not a reward for the good things we have done, so none of us can boast about it. For we are God's masterpiece. He has created us anew in Christ Jesus, so we can do the good things He planned for us long ago." (Eph. 2:1-10) **The gospel is not just an explanation of a fire insurance**

policy. We are free from both the power and penalty of sin.

SPIRITUAL REGENERATION

God's regeneration program is not a rehabilitation program. The world is in the business of rehabilitation. This involves a list of do's and don'ts that must be accomplished in the flesh with the goal of some type of miraculous recovery for the better. Religion uses the same methodology with the addition of manipulation of the scriptures to justify the actions of the flesh. All earthly solutions are temporary. Even if they work we still die.

God is in the creation business. His regeneration program begins with the death of our old nature and the birth of a whole new person "in Christ". He gives us a new heart, a new mind, a new spirit and the life of Christ. The continuous TRANSFORMATION that is a part of our spiritual growth from new born babies to mature adult sons will not be easy because even though we are righteous, complete, and holy in Christ we are still housed in our old body. All of the previous conditioning by the world we were raised in is still present. We have been saved from the power and penalty of sin but not from the presence of sin. By the power of the Holy Spirit in us and by the faith of God we must believe God's Truth in every situation and allow Christ to live through us. The difficulties expressed by Paul in

Romans 7 will become a reality for every child of God as we move from being under law and live our lives under God's grace.

"For we know that the law is spiritual, but I am of the flesh, sold under sin. For I do not understand my own actions. For "I do not do what I want, but I do the very thing I hate. Now if I do what I do not want, I agree with the law, that it is good. So now it is no longer II who do it, but sin that dwells within me. For I know that nothing good dwells in me, that is, in my flesh. For I have the desire to do what is right, but not the ability to carry it out. For I do not do the good I want, but the evil I do not want is what I keep on doing. Now if I do what I do not want, it is no longer I who do, but sin that dwells within me.

So I find it to be a law that when I want to do right, evil lies close at hand. For I delight in the law of God in my inner being, but I see in my members another law waging war against the law of my mind and making me captive to the law of sin that dwells in my members. Wretched man that I am! Who will deliver me from this body of death? Thanks be to God through Jesus Christ our Lord! So then, I myself serve the law of God with my mind, but with my flesh I serve the law of sin." (Rom. 7:14-25)

The gospel must be applied to the inner conflict, mixed motives, confused and contradictory behavior resulting from the new creation living according to the flesh. If you can identify with the words of Paul from Romans 7 please consider that ordeal as proof that you have been delivered and are not only saved, you are being saved daily from this body of death. As you grow in His grace and are led by His Spirit you will be strengthened by the trials and tribulations of this present life but they will only make you stronger. You must remember who you are and whose you are and know that He will never leave you or forsake you. You must not let the world distract you from hearing from a Heavenly Father who loves you more than you love yourself. Immediately after receiving Jesus as Lord and Savior the best thing that could have happened to any of us would be physical death. But, God left me and you here for a purpose. That purpose was for us to glorify Him via the manifestation of the life of Christ through us in this present world. As we are transformed into the image of His Son to become the sons of God who reflect His glory. Nothing else matters.

FOCUS

"What shall we say then? Shall we continue in sin that grace may abound? Certainly not! How shall we who died to sin live any longer in it?" (Rom. 6:1-2). In order to live as ambassadors of Christ in the Kingdom of God we need to realize that being religious is not

God's plan for his children. Our relationship with our Heavenly Father is founded in our union with Christ established at the new birth and the guidance and leadership of the Holy Spirit moment by moment. By faith we are able to live and not just survive. We must understand that as new creations "in Christ" we now live in both the world and the kingdom of God simultaneously. We must do only what we see the Father doing and say only what the Father instructs us to say. Our focus must be on the heavenly and not on the natural. God's perspective must become our perspective in all things so that when the world observes and hears us they will see and hear Him.

New born Christians are mostly fixated on and worry about sin. This is because most churches teach a mixture of law and grace. The religion we are familiar with is quick to point out the do's and don'ts that are required for maintenance of one's salvation status. This religious roller coaster ride usually ends in depression and a sense of hopelessness because we end up trying and failing constantly instead of trusting. Instead of focusing on what to do about sin, focus on what God has already done that we could not do for ourselves.

"Or do you know that as many of us as were baptized into Christ Jesus were baptized into His death? Therefore, we were buried with Him through baptism into death, that just as Christ was raised from the dead by the glory of the Father, even so we also should walk in newness of life.

For if we have been united together in the likeness of His death, certainly we also shall be in the likeness of His resurrection, knowing this, that our old man was crucified with Him, that the body of sin might be done away with, that we should no longer be slaves of sin. For he who has died has been freed from sin. Now if we died with Christ, we believe that we shall also live with Him, knowing that Christ, having been raised from the dead, dies no more. Death no longer has dominion over Him. For the death that He died, he died to sin once for all; but the life that He lives, he lives to God. " (Rom.6:3-10)

Christianity is not a matter of what you do or don't do but who God has made you to be "in Christ." The gospel truth is that as new creations we must not live according to the flesh but according to the Spirit. We are to identify with both the death and resurrection of Jesus. Our new life is His life. Because we are united with Christ everything that God says about Him is also true about us. Believing the truth of God's Word is a necessity but the evidence of our proclamation is found in the practical application of that truth in our everyday lives. "Likewise you also, reckon yourselves to be dead indeed to sin, but alive to God in Christ Jesus our Lord. Therefore, do not let sin reign in your mortal body, that you should obey it in its lusts. And do not present your members as instruments of unrighteousness to sin, but present yourselves to God as being alive from the dead, and your members instruments of righteousness to God. For sin shall not have dominion over you, for you are not under law but under grace." (Rom. 6:11-14)

Sin is not just a compilation of all the acts of disobedience against a Holy God. Sin is unbelief. It is a refusal to believe what God says about who we are in Christ. The child of God who has heard the truth and still elects to live below his/her potential is living in sin. It is not our responsibility to try not to sin. Our only responsibility is to believe that we are "dead to sin and alive to God" (Rom. 6:11) and focus our attention on who God has made us to be in Christ. Until we learn to "trust and obey" we will not experience the benefits of the gospel.

WHO ARE YOU?

Your answer to this question will have a profound effect on your sanity, relationships, and all of your decisions. Your God given purpose can be fulfilled only when you can answer this question. According to personality theorist, Carl Rogers, the internal conflict and confusion that leads to personal and relational dysfunction is the result of our ignorance of a clear self-image and our concern about how we are viewed by others. If I want accurate information about my Chevy Malibu I contact the manufacturer. Likewise, a true self-image cannot be ascertained except by consulting your creator. In other words, until I know who God is I will never know who I am.

"Without FAITH it is impossible to please God" (Heb. 11:6). Our actions are the sum total of what we believe. When we believe that we are dead to sin and alive to God we are not manipulated by the false assumptions about ourselves. We are not distracted by the worlds lies and the false belief that material goods can satisfy our need for provision and protection. But the issue is that most "Christians" who have read Romans 6 over and over again still act as if they do not believe the truth of God's Word. If we are to live by faith, the truth that we believe should be evident in our behavior. The choice between a natural lifestyle of fear, guilt, and pride and the alternative lifestyle established on faith, hope and love is available to every living soul. "Therefore do not let sin reign in your mortal body that you should obey it in its lust. And do not present your members as instruments of unrighteousness to sin, but present yourselves to God as beings alive from the dead, and your members as instruments of righteousness to God. For sin shall not have dominion over you, for you are not under law but under grace" (Rom. 6:12-14).

Our confession is an expression of what we believe and when we insist on complaining about what we don't have and what we still want we exhibit the natural lifestyle. How can we say we trust God while complaining about our condition and blaming everyone and everything, including God, for our station in this life? There are many Christians who will not claim their inheritance in this life but would rather remain in the nursery room of religion and use the excuse "I am just a sinner saved by grace" while they continue to beg men for temporary assistance and pray to God for what He has already supplied. We seek happiness in this world while ignoring God altogether. Many fail to understand the difference between happiness and joy and would find it difficult to explain the difference if confronted with the question.

According to Augustine the happy life is based on truth. It is possible to be happy and not have joy. I don't believe that it is possible to experience true joy and not be happy. True joy comes only from union with God who is the source of all good things. His unconditional love never fails and we can never be separated from His care. Yet, we don't always experience that union in this life because we only know Him via faith and hope. His love is certain and has been proven by the cross. If true joy and happiness is based on the apprehension of faith in Him and hope in the future He has promised, where does that leave you in the scheme of things?

"Blessed be the God and Father of our Lord Jesus Christ, who has blessed us with every spiritual blessing in the heavenly places." (Ehp.1:3) The eternal Father has always been, is now, and always will be the eternal source of joy and happiness. That means that everything one needs for happiness has always been available. The requirement for experiencing the alternative lifestyle of grace is to accept the truth and thank God that in Christ we are holy, righteous, acceptable, forgiven, adequate, perfect and complete. This is the confession of those who are alive to God and dead to sin. As children of God when we believe the gospel about who we are in

62

Christ we are empowered to live the alternative lifestyle, led by the Spirit, operating in FAITH, and inspired by HOPE while we allow our Father to use us to be Christ to others. The transformation process facilitates our being saved daily from the lifestyle of Law to a lifestyle of grace.

"Stand fast therefore in the liberty by which Christ has made us free, and do not be entangled again with a yoke of bondage. Indeed, I, Paul, say to you that if you become circumcised, Christ will profit you nothing. And I testify again to every man who becomes circumcised that he is a debtor to keep the whole law. You have become estranged from Christ, you who attempt to be

justified by law, you have fallen from grace. For we through the Spirit eagerly wait for the hope of righteousness by faith. For in Christ Jesus neither circumcision nor uncircumcision avails anything, but faith working through love" (Gal. 5:1-6). The Christian life is not you and me trying our best to live up to God's perfect standard. It is the life of Christ manifested through the believer by the power of the Holy Spirit through an obedient response to the God's Word. It is Christ living through us. It is FREEDOM as a result of His investment in us. It is evidenced not by proclamation but by application as the fruit of the Spirit becomes visible in our lives. **"But the fruit of the Spirit is love,**

joy, peace, longsuffering, kindness, goodness, faithfulness, gentleness, self-control. Against such there is no law. And those who are Christ's have crucified the flesh with its passions and desires. If we live in the Spirit, let us also walk in the Spirit. Let us not become conceited, provoking one another, envying one another" (Gal.5:22-26).

We spend most of our lives functioning at a level of dysfunction that accepts the path of least resistance in our quest to survive and feel "normal" in a world that ignores the fact that it has been judged and sentenced to death. Mankind still actually believes that "he who dies with the most toys wins." We try to impress everyone, including God, and when we fail we feel insecure and worthless.

Imagine what would happen and how different our lives would be if we allow God to use us to fulfill the purpose for which we were created. What would happen if you stopped trying to fix everything and everybody, including yourself, and trusted our eternal Father for your provision and protection in every area of your life? Since death and life are in the power of the tongue what would happen if you only said what God says about you instead of what you think based on what you don't know about yourself or what others say about you? How different would your conversation be if you replaced criticizing and complaining about others with encouraging and praying for them? What would your world look like if when everyone in your world saw and heard you they heard and saw Jesus? When others see you now who do they see...Jesus or you?

SHUT UP! GIVE UP! GROW UP! GET UP & GO!

Several years ago when I was at a crossroads in my ministry the Lord spoke to me with some personal instruction designed to help me move forward. I received the understanding that this short message to me could be both the shortest and longest sermon message that the Spirit could deliver through me. If you examine each part of the proclamation you will also discover that there is no sermon of substance that does not fit into one of the four categories. Full obedience to this given revelation required an intentional effort, on my part, to recognize the presence of Almighty God in every area of my life and total submission to His plan and purpose for my life. I believe that you will agree that this will also apply to your personal relationship with a loving Heavenly Father who wants your commitment to His will for your life to be intentional.

SHUT UP!

One of our common human flaws is that we talk and think too much. This would not be a problem if we had complete knowledge of a subject before we engaged in conversation with positive intentions. We also often over think subjects, situations, and circumstances in an attempt to resolve issues that we are either unqualified or ill equipped to address. Most of our conversations are initiated via fear, guilt or pride and we often find ourselves in the middle of a dialogue we never should have begun if we had thought about what we said before we said it. Our selfishness and pride prompts us to defend ourselves, blow our own horn, or undermine the reputation of someone else so that we can look good in our own eyes or the eyes of others. There is scientific proof that eighty-two percent of the conversations we have on a daily basis are conversations we have with ourselves. "Self-talk" is the term used to describe this activity. You may be surprised to learn that ninety percent of that eighty-two percent is negative conversation. That's right! Ninety percent of what we say to ourselves about ourselves or about others is negative.

"Death and life are in the power of the tongue: and they that love it shall eat the fruit thereof" (Prov. 18:21). Our words are powerful. God created an entire world by speaking it into existence. Because we are made in His image we function in the same manner. The words we speak have a profound relationship to our destiny because they represent what we are thinking. Our conversation reveals our true perspective as it relates to our world view. We either function as God's children whose kingdom perspective is led by the Holy Spirit and grounded in God's Word, or we live in a constant state of dysfunction guided by the natural world system with its lies, temptations, and confusion. The first step in the transformation process afforded by salvation is to realize that one who does not know Jesus does not know anything. A spiritual aptitude is not necessary to come to the realization that silence is the wisest choice for the concealment of ignorance. Every living soul was born innocent but confused and ignorant of the truth. Raised in a world that by nature feeds on dysfunction, we were taught how to navigate the darkness by dysfunctional parents, educated in a dysfunctional educational system, and required to submit to a dysfunctional system of government. I use this analogy to explain that any parental, educational, or governmental system that leaves Almighty God out of the decision making process is dysfunctional. We learn the language of the world and the culture in which we were raised and because we learn to live without the Truth we actually believe that we can protect ourselves, provide for ourselves and be satisfied with our own self efforts. At an early age we make premature cognitive commitments to concepts and beliefs that prove untrue and even harmful as we mature but continue to say the same things to our children and

ourselves as we continue in our
natural insanity.

The first step in hearing from God
is to SHUT UP! If God is speaking
to you is there anything more
important than what He has to
say? Is there anything more
important to think about than what
God is saying to you? Imagine,
God loves you enough to stop you
in your tracks and offer you
everything you need to correct
your confusion and dysfunction.
Unbelievable? Believe it! The only
problem is that you are probably
not going to like what He has to
say. His instructions are not going
to make sense. The world you have
been raised in has you so messed
up that God's truth will sound
insane. You will have to exercise
the faith you have always used but

now you will have to place that
'mustard seed' faith in a God you
cannot see except in the face and
acts of His children. Before you are
spiritually mature enough for God
to speak through you, you must
learn to listen to His voice. In
Christ you have everything you
need to be and to do what He ask
of you. You will just have to learn
how to use His gifts. "For God has
not given us a spirit of fear, but of
power and of love and of a sound
mind" (2 Tim. 1:7). The
resurrection power of the Holy
Spirit will lead you out of
dysfunction and confusion and into
a peace that cannot be understood
if you just learn first to SHUT UP!

GIVE UP!

Here is an important truth for you to remember. You are not, have not ever been, and never will be IN CHARGE. The proof is that everyone has to answer to someone. No matter how high up the latter you climb there is always someone above you. The Bible is a book containing a series of love letters from God to you. There are sixty-six letters total. I always say that sixty-five of those letters were purposed to let you know that you don't have to experience the flames of hell. God wants to love the hell out of you. If you are still not convinced there is one last letter that should scare the hell out of you. As you read the Bible it is evident that God never gives up

His pursuit of the creatures He made in His image. This is because before He created the world and everything in it God made a covenant with Himself that He would have sons. God not only swore to Himself that He would have sons but made total provision for mankind and the accomplishment of His will before he created man. God's work will be finished when a holy nation of priest receives the benefits of God's promise to Himself (Rev. 13:8). All you have to do is GIVE UP what you cannot keep for what God has done for you.

We are all victims of the same dysfunction. We actually believe that we can fix ourselves without God's help. I hear presidential candidates making promises about what they can do for us and what we can do as a nation to solve the problems we have created. The spiritual component of problem solving is totally ignored and almost never mentioned. The proof of our dysfunction and insanity is that we keep doing the same thing over and over again and expecting different results. When will we learn to trust God? When will we stop trying to solve everyone's issues except our own? Even when we finally accept the salvation offered by The Father we still would rather engage in religious rehabilitation than believe that Jesus paid the price in full and we can rest in that knowledge.

According to Rom. 6 all true believers have been delivered from the power and penalty of sin. We identity not only with Jesus in His death but also in His resurrection. "Therefore we are buried with Him by baptism into death that like as Christ was raised up from the dead by the glory of the Father, even so we also should walk in newness of life." (Rom.6:4) By faith we must believe that we are new creations in Christ and that we are dead to sin and alive to God. We must live our lives as if we died and were raised from the dead and this new life is actually the life of Christ. As new creations united with Christ we are equipped to fulfill our destiny as we are transformed into His image. "And do not present your members as instruments of unrighteousness to sin, but present yourselves to God as being alive from the dead, and your members as instruments of righteousness to God" (Rom.6:13-14).

Based on God's mercy we are to give up playing God and present our bodies as living sacrifices, serving and obeying Him by the power of the Holy Spirit. He has made us holy and acceptable in His sight and our only reasonable service is to make ourselves available for His plan and purpose for our lives. Instead of being molded by the values of this world we are transformed and changed by the renewing of our minds. When we learn to think right we also learn to act in a manner that reflects the character of Christ. Once we learn to shut up and give up we can then GROW UP.

GROW UP!

"For though by this time you ought to be teachers, you have need again for someone to teach you the elementary principles of the oracles of God, and you have come to need milk and not solid food. For everyone who partakes only of milk is not accustomed to the word of righteousness, for he is an infant. But solid food is for the mature, who because of practice have their senses trained to discern good and evil." (Heb. 5:12-14)

No parent expects their child to remain an infant forever. The process of growth includes not only physical but emotional and intellectual development. At some point our children are expected to become responsible and accountable adults who are then equipped to raise and nurture their own children. Spiritual growth is no different and the transformation from infant (nepios) to a full grown son of God (huios) is the responsibility of the indwelling Holy Spirit and is evidenced by the manifestation of the character of Christ in our daily lives. Spiritual maturity is a critical issue in the body of Christ because as we mature both as individuals and as a corporate son of God we advance closer to our destiny. The writer of Hebrews reminds us that unless we understand the daily workings of the elementary principles in our lives we will never be able to receive the deeper things ordained for the fulfillment or our individual destinies.

On the street where I live there are at least four residences that also serve as day care centers. One of these even specializes in children with handicaps. Another operates 24 hours daily. All of them fulfill the same purpose. Parents drop their children at these facilities to be taken care of while they go about their day working and doing whatever they do to provide for themselves and their families. These facilities are professional "baby sitters" that serve to provide for and protect these infants during the time they are there.
Reasonable discipline is the only

thing expected from these children. Once they become old enough to be enrolled in the school system they are removed from the authority of the "baby sitter" and new expectations are initiated as it relates to both the child and the "teacher." As the child advances through the system their growth is accompanied through both responsibility and accountability. These children grow up to become young adults and then hopefully mature and responsible adults. This is not necessarily true in the church as it relates to spiritual growth.

Because we have failed to realize that the Christian faith is not a religion but a relationship with Almighty God, many churches serve primarily as "day care

centers." Newly born again
Christians are allowed to remain in
that condition until they are ready
to go to heaven and in the
meantime are manipulated by an
insecure and incomplete religion
that keeps them at the foot of the
cross begging for Jesus to do for
them what He has already done.
An effective discipleship program
can rarely be found and "Sonship"
is a subject that is almost never
discussed. The elementary
doctrines (Heb. 6:1-2) remain the
focus of every message but never
with an understanding necessary to
move past that beginning phase
and those with a desire to grow
deeper in their faith are left to
themselves to discover that path.
The end result is children raising

children and the blind leading the blind.

Parenting is probably the most difficult job in the universe. The reason is that it is impossible to be an effective parent without divine guidance. God, The Father of everything, by the power of His Holy Spirit must guide and direct every step of the parenting process. Parenting requires unconditional love and the source of that love is Christ in you, the hope of glory. We do not begin to grow until we begin to grow spiritually. The transformation process involves discipleship. It requires mature, spiritual fathers (and mothers) who have an unwavering trust in God and are committed to being Christ to others. It requires sacrifice and an

unselfish attitude. It requires
spiritual discernment and the
ability to see everything from an
eternal perspective. It requires that
we become fully mature spiritual
adults who pray for and believe for
those who are still as immature
and dysfunctional as we once were.
It requires that we stop being
distracted by the world, focus on
the Word and GROW UP.

THE MIRACLE OF COMMUNICATION

God created man with the intent of
having sons who would be both
informed and equipped by Him to
reflect His character. Even though
the death and resurrection of Jesus
restored man to his position as
God's son he retains the culture of

an orphan after new birth. Most born again Christians fail to relate to God as Father because the culture of the orphan filters the voice of God in His attempt to speak to man directly…. Spirit to spirit. Communication, even for born again Christians, is difficult because the clarity of God's communication with man was distorted by the preeminence of the mind of the soul at the fall of man.

In the beginning there was a flawless communication between God and man. Since man was created as a spiritual being with a soul and a body it is possible that the conversations between God and Adam may not have been vocal. However, since God spoke the world into existence and gave man that same ability I suppose it was not wasted. I often wonder what that language sounded like. God, who is Spirit, spoke to man's spirit. Man's soul was subservient to his spirit and his body just followed directions. For Adam, communication was a spiritual experience and his only view of reality was the same as his Father's. Once man sinned the eyes of his soul were opened and the result was a distorted and misinformed view of reality.

God was and is committed to the establishment of a holy nation of priest via the precreation covenant (Rom.13:8). His plan included the ways by which creation would speak to man's soul and furnish a continual source of information designed to remind man of His intentions. "For since the creation of the world God's invisible qualities—his eternal power and divine nature—have been clearly seen, being understood from what has been made, so that men are without excuse" (Rom. 1:20). As members of the Adam's family God could only expect a response from man that would be limited by his uninformed soul. Man could recognize the symbols, types, shadows, and analogies present in creation but could not see the purpose or intent behind them. "Now we see but a poor reflection as in a mirror; then we shall see face to face. Now I know in part; then I shall know fully, even as I am fully known." (1 Co.13:12) Before the restoration of God's communion with man's spirit he spoke to man through prophetic utterances, dreams, visions and parables. "Long ago, at many times and in many ways, God spoke to our fathers by the prophets, 2 but in these last days he has spoken to us by his Son, whom he appointed the heir of all things, through whom also he created the world. 3 He is the radiance of the glory of God and the exact imprint of his nature, and he upholds the universe by the word of his power. After making purification for sins, he sat down at the right hand of the Majesty on high, 4 having become as much superior to angels as the name he has inherited is more excellent than theirs." (Heb.1:1-4)

God speaks to man today but He only speaks to His sons. He only

speaks through His sons. He
speaks to us through His Word. He
communicates with us Spirit to
spirit. He does not speak to your
head but to your heart. Your new
heart. As a new creation in Christ a
son of God is able to hear from his
Father via the Holy Spirit whose
purpose is not only to empower
you but to raise you up and
conform you to the image of
Christ. His attempt to communicate
with us is often distorted by our
own voice. We naturally either talk
too much or think too much. We
try to intellectualize everything so
that we may understand what He is
saying to us. We attempt to
understand it before we hear it.
Faith does not work that way. We
even instruct others based on our
worldly understanding of spiritual

concepts and expect them to accept our way of understanding a matter. We fail to realize that we were all created by God as unique individuals and that He has a purpose and destiny for each one of us. When we allow Him to guide and direct us individually the corporate body of Christ functions as intended because He is in charge and not us.

If you listen to yourself and the conversation of others you will come to realize why communication is so difficult. Our focus is revealed by our conversations and usually what we are focused on is ourselves. We complain about others and their short comings. We criticize them for not doing what we would do or say what we would say the exact way we would say it. We judge everything and everyone based on our carnal understanding without consulting the mind of Christ in a matter. We are quick to condemn and lacking in the forgiveness that God did not hesitate to extend to us. When it comes to our relationship with our Heavenly Father we would rather Google Him than relate to Him as a loving Father who want to meet our every need. When we go to Him it is for what we can get without consideration of what we can give. It's all about us and because of that we cannot love others as He loved us because sacrifice and suffering are required in that endeavor. Brother to brother communication is difficult if not impossible because we prefer to talk at each other rather than to each other from an eternal perspective rather than a linear one. Brother to brother communication is impossible when there is no willing and loving communication with The Father.

The spiritual principle of agreement does not require us to agree with each other but to agree with God on everything. Unless we agree with Him we are both wrong because He is the only one who is always right. In the fourth chapter of Philippians Paul appealed to Euodia and Syntyche, who he described as belonging to the Lord, to settle their disagreement and get on the same page. He was asking them to quit focusing on being right and focus on their

relationship as sister "in Christ."
"Always be full of joy in the Lord. I say it again—rejoice! 5Let everyone see that you are considerate in all you do. Remember, the Lord is coming

soon.   6Don't worry about anything; instead, pray about everything. Tell God what you need, and thank him for all he has done. 7Then you will experience God's peace, which exceeds anything we can understand. His peace will guard your hearts and minds as you live in Christ Jesus. 8And now, dear brothers and sisters, one final thing. Fix your thoughts on what is true, and honorable, and right, and pure, and lovely, and admirable. Think about things that are excellent and worthy of praise. 9Keep putting into practice all you learned and received from me—everything you heard from me and saw me doing. Then the God of peace will be with you." (Phil.4:4-8)

When we focus on ourselves confusion is inevitable because our needs and wants are the number one priority even under good intentions. When we focus on Christ and what He has done for us that we could not do for ourselves we only thank God and experience the peace and joy that exceeds anything we can understand. We then pray for and encourage others and leave the matter in the hands of our Father. We don't have to stress and strain or fuss and complain because we have prayed for our brother and committed ourselves to allow God to use us in any way He deems necessary to be Christ to those who need to see Him with skin on. Instead of thinking negative thoughts about ourselves or others we intentionally think about those things that are honorable, and right, and pure, and lovely, and admirable. Godly communication is not only Him communicating to us but through us. It is part of the character of a mature son of God.

I believe that one of the reasons that we have difficulty communicating is that we fail to realize that as newly born again creatures we not only have a new life but a new language. We are no longer human beings but are now true spiritual beings encased in a body of flesh. We are sons of God and represent the kingdom of heaven on earth. We have the privilege of seeing everything from an eternal perspective and have a unique advantage over those who are still in the dark. We are ambassadors of Christ who have the capacity to manifest the character of Christ and function as a royal priesthood and a holy nation. We are commissioned to go and make disciples by bringing the light of the gospel of the kingdom to those who are enslaved by sin and darkness. This gospel is the same message that Jesus preached and the salvation it offers must be

understood within the context of
the kingdom of God.

THE WRONG GOSPEL

*"In our day again the gospel of the
kingdom has been replaced by an
inadequate and false gospel, a
gospel of personal peace and well-
being. This false gospel loads
believers with false assurances
about their eternal state, even as it
distracts them from the pursuit of
holiness, minimizes the life of
discipline and obedience, fosters an
idolatry of material success,
redefines the "go/tell" mission of
the church, and leaves the larger
issues of culture and society in the
hands of the children of the
kingdom of darkness.*

The gospel of the kingdom has become captive to mere personal interest, felt needs, aspirations of prosperity, postmodern relativism, and social and political ambitions. Certainly there are aspects of most of these in the gospel of the kingdom: however, the gospel of the kingdom is much broader, much deeper, much more integrated, and much more sweeping in its implications and power than any or all its present-day substitutes. What we need today is a movement to restore the gospel of the kingdom—Christianity as a worldview – to the churches and the public square. This will not happen without the deliberate, coordinated effort of those who share a burden for such a broad and deep renewal." Vishal

Mangalwadi (*Truth & Transformation...a manifesto for ailing nations*)

If you are like me, you had the same experience that most Christians have suffered through before discovering that there is something more than just church on Sundays. At some point after you "joined the church" you became discouraged by the routine of living a life of trying to be obedient to the Law and the doctrines of your church but never being able to consistently succeed at that endeavor. I kept trying to "be good" and follow the rules but Romans chapter 7 became the theme for my life. Nobody was able to explain to me the elementary doctrines of the faith (Heb. 6:1-2) with enough clarity to allow me to gain the understanding that would allow me to move on to the deeper truths that God want to share with me to bring an awareness of the destiny He planned for me. The church functioned much like the world and I was expected to attain a level of perfection for which I had no examples in the flesh. I was still making the same mistakes and living two lives and it was easy to hide my faults from church members who were in the same boat as I was. In fact, I really had no problem being the same me I used to be until I realized that that was not God's intent and that He had a better plan for me. I kept thinking about heaven while living according to the world. I kept trying to live my life according to 10 commandments because the church told me that that was God's desire for my life. When I realized that I could not reach that level of perfection I was told that either I did not have enough faith or that I should keep praying about it.

Schizophrenia is a mental condition that interferes with the ability to think clearly, manage emotions, make decisions, and relate to others. Medical technicians identify the causes as genetics, environment, brain chemistry and substance abuse. Science says there is no cure but the condition can be treated by psychotherapy and drugs.

From a spiritual perspective we are all schizophrenic. One cannot be religious and not suffer from this condition because religion is man's substitute for God's plan for a relationship with His sons. We are born that way. The dysfunctional lifestyle of all who are born in sin is evidenced by the symptoms that identify this condition. We are all born into the Adams family and into a sinful environment and substance abuse is more common than we would like to admit. Even when we accept God's Truth and believe in the kingdom of God we continue to try to live in the earth in the same way that unbelievers live. The incomplete gospel that most of us have received has not equipped us for life in the kingdom. The majority of born again Christians have no concept of a life supported by the authority of Jesus Christ and lived out in the context of the body of Christ, the purpose and direction of that life being ruled and governed by the Holy Spirit. We say we trust God and yet still eat from the tree of the knowledge of good and evil.

Jesus preached the gospel of the kingdom and charged us with the same task. The gospel of salvation is not the complete gospel when it is not offered within the context of life in the kingdom once saved.

"Praise be to the God and Father of our Lord Jesus Christ, who has blessed us in the heavenly realms with every spiritual blessing in Christ. For He chose us in Him before the creation of the world to be holy and blameless in His sight. In love He predestined us to be adopted as His sons through Jesus Christ in accordance with His pleasure and will – to the praise of His glorious grace, which He has freely given us in the One He loves." (Eph. 1:3-6) According to God's Word the kingdom of God was ordained from the foundations

of the world and those who elect to become sons of God and members of the body of Christ have already received the benefits of God's pre-creation covenant with Himself. As sons we are now a part of the kingdom and the kingdom is in us via the Holy Spirit. You are predestined to be conformed to a destiny known in the mind of God before you were in your mother's womb.

The kingdom of heaven verifies that we are eternal beings in time and the kingdom of God indicates that our eternal existence in time enjoys the full extent of support that comes from the throne of God. The kingdom of God is an eternal reality and as ambassadors of Christ we are blessed with the capacity to manifest His character, preach the Truth, and fulfill our God-ordained destinies by the

power and presence of the Holy
Spirit in us.

GOD'S INTENT AND OURS

Let me be clear. God's original
intent was, and still is, to have
sons who will glorify Him and
reflect His glory. It is up to each
one of us to decide is we will
accept His invitation of sonship and
the benefits that accompany that
decision. All we have to do is
repent of a lifestyle of sin and
death under the lordship of Satan
and accept the salvation of the
cross. Jesus did all that needs to
be done and the price for man's
freedom from sin and death has
been paid. There is no
rehabilitation for a dead man. This
new life that we receive is the life
of Christ and it is not to be wasted.

This new life allows the sons of God to be Christ to others.

Believing the Truth about who God is and who you are in Christ becomes visible by your works, not your proclamation. When the Holy Spirit is in control the soul must submit to the revelation knowledge and wisdom that God only shares with His sons. Suffering is a daily companion of the maturing son. Like Jesus, we must sacrifice any desire to do things our way and be intentional in our submission to the will of God in everything. Like Jesus, we must become containers for the use of The Father in the completion of His plan and purpose. Like Jesus, we must become intentional in listening to those who are seeking the light and to the Holy Spirit for instructions before we respond to their cries. Like Jesus, we must see others as God sees them and then let them see Him through us. All that is in us that still looks like us must die so that we may be transformed into the image of Christ and we must intentionally submit to that process as it progresses. Why?

Once we learn to shut up, give up, and grow up we become useful in the hands of God. It is then that we must **GET UP AND GO** because the Christian life is not passive. As ambassadors of Christ in the kingdom of God we are commissioned to represent the King. The way we live is a Spirit led journey from new birth to spiritual adulthood. As sons of God we understand that salvation is not about going to heaven because heaven is a benefit of being removed from the kingdom of darkness into the kingdom of light.

We are not preoccupied with getting folk saved because we cannot save anyone. What we are committed to is the obedience necessary for the transformational process to produce in us the exact representation of the nature and character of Christ.

On the evening of that day, the first day of the week, the doors being locked where the disciples were for fear of the Jews, Jesus came and stood among them and said to them, "Peace be with you." **20** When he had said this, he showed them his hands and his side. Then the disciples were glad when they saw the Lord. **21** Jesus said to them again, "Peace be with you. As the Father has sent me, even so I am sending you." **22** And when he had said this, he breathed on them and said to them, "Receive the Holy Spirit. *23 **If you forgive the sins of any, they are forgiven them; if you withhold forgiveness from any, it is withheld.**"* (John 20:20-23)

Did you happen to notice verse 23? Jesus instructed His disciples to forgive the sins of those who are still ignorant of the truth. Say what? This may be a surprise and kind of scary but this scripture informs us that as sons of God who are in Christ we are authorized to inform sinners that their sins have been forgiven. Read Romans 6 if you don't believe this. We are not equal with God and we are not independent representatives either. It is not our responsibility to engage our flesh in an effort to do something for God but to become the exact representation of His goodness, His compassion, His mercy and His decision in every situation, circumstance and encounter. As ambassadors of the kingdom we do not have a vote or an opinion. We are vessels offered for His plan and purpose. *"I appeal to you therefore, brothers, by the mercies of God, to present your bodies as a living sacrifice, holy and acceptable to God, which is your spiritual worship,] 2 Do not be conformed to this world, but be transformed by the renewal of your mind, that by testing you may discern what is the will of God, what is good and acceptable and perfect." (Rom.12:1-2)*

There has only been one perfect life and that is the life of Jesus. We have the awesome opportunity of receiving His life and allowing Him to live and continue God's plan of sonship. As sons of God the kingdom of God is within us and like Jesus we are empowered to do and say what we see the Father doing and saying. Kingdom rule is not a democracy. As new creations in Christ we can apply the truth to our new lives by using the new heart and mind that came with rebirth. It is not about us. It is all about Jesus. "Let this mind be in you which was also in Christ Jesus, who, being in the form of God, did not consider it robbery to be equal with God, but made Himself of no reputation, taking the form of a bondservant, and coming in the likeness of men. And being found in appearance as a man, He

Humbled Himself and became obedient to the point of death, even the death of the cross. Therefore God also has highly exalted Him and given him the name which is above every name, that at the name of Jesus every knee should bow, of those in heaven, and of those on earth, and of those under the earth, and that every tongue should confess that Jesus Christ is Lord, to the glory of God the Father." (Phil.2:5-11)

The purpose of the kingdom is not to secure fame and fortune in the earth. God gives us everything we need so that we never have to worry about provision and protection. Our purpose is to represent the Living God both individually and corporately as we are formed into a community that defies all reason and history by loving each other as Christ loved us. By being Christ to others. By the power of the Holy Spirit we intentionally resist the temptations and influence of our natural cultures and submit to the culture of the kingdom of God.

The intentionality spoken of in this book is not just about you doing something important with your life but more about doing what God intended for you to do. Law and religion cannot help you reach the destiny God ordained for you before you were in your mother's womb. Ultimately what God wants is to be Himself through you. LET HIM!

Made in the USA
Columbia, SC
08 March 2023

13398697R00065